About the Author

TONY BUZAN is considered to be one of the world's leading authorities on learning techniques. His training company, The Learning Methods Group, advises middle- and top-management executives of such corporations as IBM, 3M, Encyclopedia Britannica, and Mobil. Buzan has received numerous industry awards, and several BBC television programs have been created around his learning techniques, among them a ten-part series called *Use Your Head*, which was the basis for Buzan's book *Use Both Sides of Your Brain*. Mr. Buzan is also the author of *Speed Reading* and *Speed Memory*, among others.

THE
BRAIN USER'S
GUIDE

TONY BUZAN

THE BRAIN USER'S GUIDE

A Handbook for Sorting Out Your Life

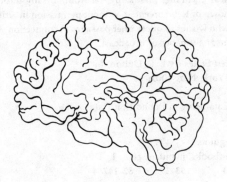

E. P. DUTTON, INC.   NEW YORK

Published in the United States by E. P. Dutton, Inc.,
2 Park Avenue, New York, N.Y. 10016

Library of Congress Cataloging in Publication Data

Buzan, Tony.
    The brain user's guide.
    1. Success—Handbooks, manuals, etc.   I. Title.
BF637.S8B88   1983   158'.1   82-14764

DRAWINGS BY LORRAINE GILL
TYPOGRAPHY BY EARL TIDWELL

ISBN: 0-525-48045-5
Published simultaneously in Canada by Clarke, Irwin & Company Limited,
Toronto and Vancouver

10 9 8 7 6 5 4 3 2 1

First Edition

Contents

Introduction   *vii*

1 Laying the Groundwork for Change   *1*
    The exercises: an introduction   *2*
    Changing habits   *3*
    The new knowledge about your brain   *4*

2 The Left and Right Brain
    and Other New Discoveries about You   *6*
    Left-brain, right-brain check   *9*
    The rest/activity cycle   *10*
    The ghost hobby   *11*
    Recall versus understanding   *13*
    Pace change   *13*
    Serendipity   *15*
    Chunking, self-development,
        and the need for love   *16*

3 Self-exploration and Organization   *17*
    Exercise 1. Obituary writer   *17*
    Exercise 2. Your personal Life Expectancy
                Questionnaire   *22*
    Exercise 3. Self-analysis   *27*
    Exercise 4. Your "To Do" List   *29*
    Exercise 5. Your Ideal Future   *35*

vi

4 Divide and Conquer   37
Exercise 1. List memory   37
Exercise 2. Number/calculation/
memory exercise   41
Chunking exercise analysis   42
Gaining control of yourself   43
Exercise 3. Self-chunking   43
The need for love and friendship   47
Self-development   49
Financial self-management   54
Financial analysis   56
Selecting your remaining divisions   62
Exercise 4. Ranking reality; ranking ideal   63
Organizing your seven or fewer
Major Divisions   65

5 Advice for the future   123
In conclusion   129

Introduction

I have often been asked how I initially became involved in the field of brain research, and what were the specific steps that led me from this involvement to my current interest in the relationship between information on the human brain and the day-to-day, year-to-year problems of self-management.

The story starts in a British junior school in 1949, when I was seven years old. At that time my best friend and I were interested in nature study and little else. After school (and sometimes when we stayed away from school!), we would spend all our time in the fields and by streams, absorbing nature as only children can do. One day we had what the teacher called a test, in which we were asked simple questions about the world around us, such as, "What's the difference between a butterfly and a moth?" "Name three fishes you can find in the local streams," and so on. My friend, who could identify birds by their flight patterns, scored zero. I, who could not, scored 100.

The school labeled me intelligent and him dumb, whereas we both knew that in the real knowledge of nature the roles were reversed. We sensed on one level and knew on another that something was wrong, but neither of us could identify it.

Only years later did I realize that it was simply a matter of literacy (he was illiterate), and only recently did I realize that the differences between us were identifiable as differences in the use of our left and right brains. My friend's problem, if it can be so called, was that certain abilities handled by the left side of his brain had not been properly developed, and as such he was not able to "manage" certain activities. His was a basic problem in self-management.

As I continued my studies, eventually teaching at schools, in universities, and in the business arena, I became increasingly aware of the universality of certain problems, and of the constant relationship of the problems to basic lack of awareness of, or training in, certain brain skills.

Everywhere people complain of poor concentration; ill health; vague feelings of dissatisfaction; weak memory; inadequate and incomplete personal relationships; fear of financial inadequacy; stress from an excessive volume of work or things to do; general lack of direction; an inability to manage time; and the rarity of times of real peace, relaxation, and happiness.

Myths abound to support our beliefs in the inevitability of these problems:

- "Memory gets worse and brain cells drop off as you get older." This is not true.
- "The brain has a limited capacity." This is increasingly thought to be untrue.
- "Broke and happy." I've observed that "broke" people are among the unhappiest that I know.

Why are so many people tired so much of the time? Why are so many people always behind? In the wrong job? Unable to start things? Why are so many others unable to finish those things they've started? Why do they waste so much time? Why do so many people live such fragmented and unsatisfactory lives?

As I pondered these questions, I asked myself the same questions about my own life. Before I began to relate brain research to time management, my own self-management systems were a shambles. Scraps of paper on which odd notes had been jotted infested my pockets and filing systems. As a result I went through many frantic searches for that one piece that was particularly important, and which was always the last to be found. The plague of odd little diaries, record books, memo pads, and writing tablets began to invade my home. The constant failure to remember the important anniversaries and dates of those I loved was a constant embarrassment and mutual hurt. And the occasional major disasters due to the scattered paths of my "organized" life began to build up increasing stress. In addition, I was increasingly cramming my time with more activity, moving faster, and going progressively nowhere.

As soon as I began to apply the latest findings about the way my brain functions, things started to improve. By managing my time more appropriately, I was able to accomplish more while feeling less fatigued; by acting on my new knowledge of the relationship between my brain and body, I was able to increase my general physical health, while at the same time improving my overall mental capacity; and by practicing self-organization based on brain theory, I was able to reduce drastically the number of those little diaries, record books, memo pads, writing tablets, and scraps of paper.

My next concern was whether self-planning was going to lead me into any number of traps. Would I become rigid? Would I have to face aspects of my own inadequacy? Would I become self-conscious, lacking in spontaneity and freedom? The surprising truth of the matter was that organizing my life gave me *greater* flexibility; made me feel *more* adequate, more *positively* self-conscious and less negatively so; and allowed me *more* freedom and spontaneity than I had had before. The reason for this

x   lay in the fact that it was the problems and their increasing effect on me that were making me rigid, inadequate, and negatively self-conscious, and leaving me no free time. As soon as I broke through their restraints, things began to improve.

       As a result of this, I began to exchange ideas with friends and colleagues, and eventually began to teach self-management and self-organization. Using this book, you will be able to go through a process that has taken me years to develop and apply to my life. The book, which was originally titled *Was Am Do Become*, can become the basis of your Life Management Program. It is designed to help you get a perspective on who you were, who you are, what you want to do, and who you are going to become.

THE
BRAIN USER'S
GUIDE

1

Laying
the Groundwork
for Change

The chapters that follow will allow you to discover the keys to:

1. Improved productivity
2. Greater self-awareness
3. More self-control and self-determination
4. The increasing satisfaction of your emotional, cultural, and spiritual needs
5. Increased physical health, with a corresponding reduction in stress and tension
6. Continuing intellectual growth

In addition to these general discoveries, you will be given specific information on how to improve:

1. Concentration
2. Personal relationships

2

3. Memory
4. Financial management
5. Creative thinking
6. Vocabulary
7. Self-confidence
8. Motivation
9. Quality of life

The book is designed for everybody and has been structured to allow you, working by and on yourself, to tailor the way in which you run your life. By the time you have completed the book, you will have developed an ongoing, self-correcting, self-organizing system, a Life Management Program.

My approach goes beyond traditional calendars and self-management systems based on simple series of priority listings. It is not a rigid grid system into which you have to fit the enormous and inevitable variety of your personal and professional life. Such systems often act only as a bandage on a sore, momentarily covering the deep-rooted problems but failing to cure the underlying cause. Over time such systems only succeed in building up negative stress.

What follows is a more flexible, comprehensive tool. It is based on the way your tremendously capable brain functions. It will enable you to get a better grip on the various elements of your life and to steer them in the direction you feel is best.

The exercises: an introduction

The exercises throughout the book will take you less than two days to complete; the results will benefit you for a lifetime. Using your own insights, you will answer such often-asked questions as, "How come nothing seems to work out right?" "What's the matter with me?" and "Isn't there more to life than *this?!*" You will be able to look forward to a life that is more in tune with who you really are and what you really want for yourself and for your family and friends. No longer will your future be one in which events, and other people, dominate you.

The path you are about to take has many exciting twists and turns, many delightful surprises, and some hard truths. You will answer fundamental questions about yourself:

WHAT HAVE I DONE?
WHO AM I?
WHAT DO I WANT TO DO?
WHO DO I REALLY WISH TO BECOME?

The process of your self-examination, though simple to describe, is by no means always easy to accomplish. Very often, when looking truthfully in your "self-mirror," you'll want to say, "That isn't me."

It is usually difficult to face an unpleasant truth, but in the long term the benefits that can result from doing so can be great. The short-term stress is positive; it gives you the energy to change and improve.

Changing habits

In the process of your own self-management and self-development you will inevitably change certain habits. This may cause other problems to loom large in the short-term—problems which your habits have kept submerged and which were the original reasons for acquiring those habits.

To give a common but important example, the majority of people who smoke start the habit in order to conceal feelings of social inadequacy, not knowing what to do with their hands, needing something to keep them occupied in embarrassing pauses, and so on; over a period of years a habit can become an involved and complex ritual.

One woman acquaintance of mine, who had been smoking

4   for years, finally stopped. When she did, she found that her feelings of social inadequacy were magnified tenfold, and she became literally frantic because she no longer had her prop. This *apparent* regression was in fact a positive event, for it allowed her to focus on the real and underlying causes for her emotions, and to approach the problem head-on rather than avoiding it for the rest of her life. She now neither smokes *nor* feels socially inadequate.

If you find yourself in similar situations, rest assured that the short-term pain is worth the long-term advantage.

The new knowledge about your brain

In order to achieve change in the direction you want, it will be helpful for you to apply some newly discovered knowledge about the way your brain and your body function, such as:

1. The different functioning systems of the left and right hemispheres (sides) of your brain
2. The difference between your memory and your understanding, and how appreciating this difference can help you manage your time far more effectively
3. The nature of the necessary rest/activity cycle of the human organism
4. The release of the brain's pressure valves, provided by your "ghost hobby": that daydream of what you always have wanted to be, or the hobby you have promised yourself you would one day take up, but never have
5. The nature of effective change of pace
6. The importance of serendipity in releasing the pressure valves mentioned above
7. The importance of other specific aspects of self-development, such as vocabulary improvement, for balancing the right and left hemispheres

8. Self-organization and the principle of "chunk-   5
   ing"—the need for your brain to organize
   things in packages that are easily handled
9. The need for love

In the next chapter we will explore a number of these areas in detail, after which a series of exercises will enable you to apply them to managing your own future successfully.

2

The Left and Right Brain

AND OTHER NEW DISCOVERIES ABOUT YOU

The Nobel prize was recently awarded to the American psychologist Roger Sperry for his breakthrough work on the two sides of the upper brain, or cortex (the part of the brain that developed only recently in evolution, which deals with more advanced intellectual functions and which is common to the higher mammals and mankind). Sperry discovered that functionally we really have *two* upper brains, and that each one, acting in harmony with the other, deals with a whole range of different activities. Sperry's work has revolutionized the way we think about our own mentality, with tremendously important implications for the whole field of self-management and self-analysis. Sperry and his coresearchers discovered that the left side of your brain deals generally with the following mental areas:

6

1. Language
2. Numbers
3. Logic
4. Analysis
5. Sequencing

Sperry also discovered that while the left side of your brain is active, the right side goes into a relaxed, semimeditative alpha-wave hum. When the situation is reversed, and the right side of your brain is active, the left side of the brain goes into the same relaxed, semimeditative alpha-wave hum. The active right brain deals, on a similarly basic level, with the following and *different* mental activities:

1. Rhythm and music
2. Color
3. Imagination
4. Daydreaming
5. Spatial awareness and three-dimensionality

Subsequent experimentation has shown that virtually everyone has the full range of mental capabilities. Unfortunately, due to miseducation and misinformation, most of us tend to think of ourselves as innately skilled in only a few of these areas and inherently unskilled in the others. We compound the problem by assuming that our weaker areas are forever unobtainable. A more accurate self-description would be, "I have developed *these* areas of my potential ability, while for various reasons I have left *those* areas dormant for the time being."

As a result of Sperry's research, millions of individuals have started to train the incorrectly labeled "weaker" aspects of their mental abilities. They have found that those "weaker" skills, when nurtured under the direction of the right teachers, are capable of blossoming, regardless of age. They have also found that these newly developed skills feed back into previously developed skills, developing these existing skills even further. The result is a synergetic effect.

8   Further studies have shown that the great geniuses of history, leading scientists and artists such as Einstein and Picasso, were in fact not lopsided people (dominant in only one side of the brain's activities) but enormously wide-ranging in their interests and activities. The great scientists often came across their breakthrough ideas while daydreaming, and most of the great artists and musicians were found to be incredibly organized and analytical, especially in relation to their work.

For example, Einstein devised special daydreaming imagination games, which he applied to his current knowledge of physics. One of these games, in which he imagined himself riding through the universe on a sunbeam, laid one of the foundation stones for his theory of relativity.

The human being who best epitomizes this balanced brain development is Leonardo da Vinci. In his time he was the world's greatest artist, sculptor, physiologist, experimenter, engineer, anatomist, and inventor. Intriguingly, the notebooks for his scientific ideas are very "right brained," containing many images in three dimension; while the final plans for his great artistic masterpieces were almost pure examples of architectural planning: straight lines, angles, numbers, and curves. Sometimes you hear the argument that the Renaissance human being is no longer possible because of the enormously increased amount of information available to us in the modern age. With the similarly rapid increase in information on the function and complexity of our human brain, it is now counterarguable that if we start to use even a small portion of our capacity, the new Renaissance human being becomes a greater possibility than ever before.

The research of Sperry and others has led to the conclusion that each one of us *needs* this balance between the left and right brain, and that if it is not achieved we become relatively ineffective.

In other words, in any self-management and self-development system it is essential to make sure that the two sides of your brain are actively balanced.

Left-brain, right-brain check

Even after hearing the evidence of Roger Sperry's research, many people still doubt that they *really* have both left-brain and right-brain abilities. To check on your left brain, simply ask yourself whether or not you can speak and understand one language. If you can, the left side of your brain is already operating far more sophisticatedly than the most modern computer. In order to have learned the language, you must have used the other left-brain skills of numeracy, logic, analysis, and sequencing. (See figure 1.)

To check on your right brain, ask yourself the question: "Where do I find myself physically located when I come up with those bursts of imaginative, creative, problem-solving ideas?"

Most people find themselves in the bathroom, taking a shower, on the toilet, or in front of the mirror, in bed, driving, or walking in the woods or by the sea. In most of these relaxed

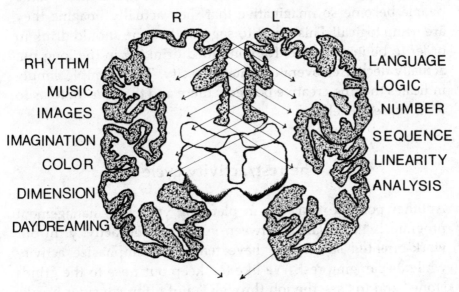

FIG. 1. *The Two Sides of the Brain*

10 and unhurried situations the individual is at ease, and usually alone. When you have such imaginative ideas, it is the right side of your brain that is functioning. And it functions best in situations like those described, during which the left side of your brain gets a well-earned rest.

You should be able to see an immediate application of the left-brain/right-brain theory to your own self-management: in doing any creative or problem-solving work, it is essential to allow the left brain to gather the information and data, and then to allow your right brain the appropriate environment, rest, and solitude in order to perform its essential part of the process.

Another right-brain check is to observe the effects of excessive alcohol. Alcohol suppresses the left-brain activities that normally keep us organized and safe in the environment, and releases those chemicals that normally hold many of our right-brain processes in appropriate check. If you feel that many people inherently have little imagination, simply reflect on their imagination after they have taken five or six stiff drinks—some people become so imaginative that they actually imagine they are being logical! This is not to suggest that one should drink in order to be imaginative, for continued drinking in the long run actually decreases overall mental capacity. The example simply indicates that the creative power is there and that it is up to us to let it express itself.

The rest/activity cycle

Another point to consider in planning your self-management program is the balance between your rest and activity. In our work-oriented society we have tended to emphasize activity while disparaging rest. We like to "keep our nose to the grindstone" and to "see the job through," and often consider breaks as a sign of laziness and sloth.

Mentally speaking, your brain can continue actively for between twenty and sixty minutes before it literally becomes drained of oxygen and physiological resources, *requiring* a rest. You can whip it like a tired horse, and it will continue, to its own—and your—detriment. As you will have realized from the previous comments on creativity and problem solving, and as you will further see when we discuss the difference between recall versus understanding, your brain requires proper management of the rest/activity cycle in order to continue to function at full force. It is an error to consider that rest is "doing nothing." Rest is a process in which your brain recuperates, reorganizes, integrates, makes things complete, and prepares for the next left-brain activity cycle.

The breaks you take can be in the form of a change of activity, in which case the hemisphere you have been using acquires its rest while you initiate activities based in the opposite hemisphere. Or it can be a full break in which you let your entire brain idle. The rest/activity cycle also contains the seeds to the solution of that ubiquitous problem: concentration.

People describe lack of concentration as one of their main mental difficulties, little realizing that those occasional or regular drifts into daydreams are actually the brain protecting itself against undue wear and tear. You *need* those little daydreams during the day. Often when you lose your concentration, it is your brain telling you that it is time to take a needed break. If you attempt to self-manage and plan without breaks, you will succeed for a short time, but in the long term you will take a different kind of break: the nervous breakdown or the physiological collapse that is the left-brained outcome of an unbalanced life.

The ghost hobby

Most people have a "ghost hobby"—that hobby they have always dreamed of taking up, but which they have put off, either through "lack of talent" or insufficient time. These ghost hob-

12   bies, the stuff of which daydreams are made, are an *essential* part of our nature. The most popular and universal ones include:

> Painting
> Playing a musical instrument
> Conducting a symphony orchestra
> Traveling (often around the world)
> Flying
> Gliding
> Diving
> Sculpting
> Craft work
> Becoming proficient in some sport

These ghost hobbies are *not* idle fantasies, but are those "untended" parts of us, begging, like Oliver Twist for more soup, for us to pay attention. As you can see, most of the ghost hobbies listed are "right-brain" activities. The reason for this appears to be that our society is left-brain dominant and does not leave enough time for such activities.

Recent research on the left and right hemispheres has shown that people who have more developed brains actually begin to use both sides for both sets of activities. As the individual becomes more skilled, all activities tend to use most of the elements from both sides of the brain. For example, sport, which was previously thought to be an "unintellectual" activity, can now be seen to include analysis, sequence, logic (and sometimes words!) from the left side of the brain, and rhythm, imagination, and dimension from the right side of the brain. The more skillful you are at a given sport, the better you're able to achieve this balance. In any self-management program it is essential to include at least one of your ghost hobbies, even if it's for only an hour a week. If you protest that you don't have time, it's even more essential!

Recall versus understanding

Most people, if they have been studying for forty minutes and are having difficulty "getting into" the material, would, if they found themselves suddenly understanding well, carry on until understanding decreased, and then take a break. Very few would take the risk of "nipping their understanding in the bud" by stopping.

However, they *should* have taken that break. The reason for this is that the brain can continue to understand well after its ability to recall or bring back that information has started to decline. If you check your own experience, you will become aware of many instances in which you understood perfectly, only to forget shortly thereafter.

If your goal is to recall something that you are studying or are in some other way involved in remembering, you must make sure that your time use is maximized. This time use coincides with the rest/activity cycle, in that a period of between twenty and sixty minutes of taking in information maximizes both understanding and recall. (See figure 2.) After sixty minutes, your understanding may continue, but recall will inevitably decline. Your break allows your brain to integrate the material already learned, and to take a mental breather before going on to the next assimilation task.

When planning your self-management system, it should become increasingly apparent that regular daily, weekly, monthly, and yearly breaks are an essential part of any effective system. And once again, the more you protest that you haven't got time for such things, the more you need to do them.

Pace change

In conjunction with balancing your brain function, taking breaks, developing ghost hobbies, and managing recall and un-

20 MINS   40 MINS   60 MINS

learning activities   and   activities ......

FIG. 2. *Learning Cycles*

derstanding, it is also important for you to vary the pace of your life. An appropriate analogy from aerobic training springs to mind: the strongest hearts are those that can continue not only for a long distance, but can also, over that distance, change the pace. This gives not only a long-term stamina but a long-term *flexible* stamina.

For example, three of the greatest 5,000 meter runners of all time, Emil Zatopek, David Bedford, and Henry Rono, shattered their opponents and existing world records by this very realization. While others were trained to run at a regular fast pace, Zatopek, Bedford, and Rono trained themselves, in addition, to put in special bursts of different speeds and durations that their more rigidly trained opponents could not handle.

Your brain requires similar changes of pace, and you can make it become both fit over the long haul *and* flexible. This does not mean letting your behavior become random, but rather

allowing for those special activities that are not part of the regu- 15
lar routine.

Serendipity

Serendipitous happenings—those spontaneous, unorganized, out-of-the-blue experiences that sometimes happen to us—are a *necessary* part of our lives. The problem with many self-management systems is that their assumptions are left-brain dominant, leaving no space for such serendipitous happenings. As a result life becomes monotonous, rigid, "colorless," and routine.

Any well-balanced personal management system *must* include the opportunity for such freewheeling time. This could include leaving certain days, weeks, months, and even years, totally open for you to do whatever you want. This might include sleeping all day, going on a bender, drifting away on your own, working your guts out on some project, visiting friends, completing a major life goal—*whatever* you feel like at the time, with no previous planning allowed.

Similarly, if you *have* carefully orchestrated and organized your life, and if some completely unexpected event throws it into a momentary shambles, don't get hyperstressed about the disruption. Flow with the momentary disruption until things have begun to settle down a bit and then allow your *flexible* management system to take up the slack.

As an example of how delightful and memorable such serendipitous moments can be, a friend of mine had a perfectly organized schedule for a business trip to Scandinavia. After having arrived somewhat jet-lagged, she got up early the following morning for an eight o'clock breakfast-plus-business-meeting. To the consternation of her hosts, the man around whom the meeting had been organized suddenly canceled, leaving my friend to wander through parks and by the seashore for the entire morning.

16   When she returned, her hosts were concerned about her reaction to the cancellation, greeting her with trepidation. In fact, she had spent one of the most peaceful and memorable mornings of her life; a window of freedom in an otherwise rigidly regimented existence had suddenly been opened to her.

Life and our intuition often offer such gifts. Rather than struggling against them, learn to accept and enjoy them.

Chunking, self-development, and the need for love

Recent findings about your brain add three key functions to the "engine room" of your Life Management Program:

1. The ability of your mind to chunk, to organize things in packages; as when you categorize things into their appropriate compartments, and when you try to associate items you are attempting to remember
2. The need for a coordinated program of self-development, including general self-management, physical health, and vocabulary improvement.
3. The necessity for love in all its various forms, both giving and receiving

After you have completed the exercises in the following chapter, we will relate these areas to your future in a more detailed manner.

3

Self-exploration and Organization

You are about to begin a series of exercises that will enable you to analyze, monitor, and change your life. As you will see, the way in which you have used, are using, and will use your brain relates intricately to each exercise. Spend as much time as you like (general guidelines will be given) and make sure you do the exercises in the order presented, completing one before moving on to the next.

Exercise 1. Obituary writer

Imagine that you are the obituary columnist for the *New York Times*, and that just as you are reading this section of the book, a telex arrives on your desk informing you of your own death, that very morning! To the telex is attached a little note from the editor requesting an immediate obituary for next morning's edition.

18   Some people need perhaps half an hour to two hours for this exercise; some prefer to mull over the obituary and the implications of their life-to-date for as much as two days to a week. Keep the length of your obituary to between the one and four pages provided.

OBITUARY

_____

_____

_____

_____

_____

_____

_____

_____

_____

_____

_____

_____

_____

_____

Obituary

Obituary

OBITUARY

Obituary writer—brief comment

If you found that your obituary was satisfactory to you, then you have a solid foundation on which to build your future. If you found that you would have liked to have contributed more to the human race to date, the remaining exercises will help you to make appropriate adjustments, and to set goals that are more in tune with your real ideals.

Exercise 2. Your personal Life Expectancy Questionnaire

The balancing of your left-brain and right-brain activities, the food you eat, the amount of exercise you take, the managing of your personal relationships, the degrees of stress to which you expose yourself, your health maintenance habits, and your overall health management affect both the quality of the life you live and the duration of your life. Now that you have examined, in the obituary exercise, who you were, fill in this questionnaire, and find out roughly how much time you have left.

Life Expectancy Questionnaire

A growing number of psychologists and physiologists believe that many of us have at birth the capacity to live to between 85 and 120. After many years of research on longevity, it is possible to give general guidelines, in the form of a questionnaire, which enable you to work out roughly how long you have to live.

Start by looking up your age in the Long-Life Table. Opposite this, you will find your basic life expectancy, derived from figures produced by insurance actuaries. Then, in answering the questions below, add to or take away from this figure, in the columns provided on page 24.

Remember one thing: women can expect to live roughly three years longer than men. Women, therefore, should add three years to start with.

THE LONG-LIFE TABLE

To answer this quiz, you first need to know your basic life expectancy. Check the table, circle your basic life expectancy, and record it in the space provided on page 24. Then answer the questions on the following pages, entering your answers on p. 24.

PRES. AGE	EST. LIFE EXPEC.	PRES. AGE	EST. LIFE EXPEC.	PRES. AGE	EST. LIFE EXPEC.
15	70.7	37	72.2	59	76.0
16	70.8	38	72.3	60	76.3
17	70.8	39	72.4	61	76.6
18	70.9	40	72.5	62	77.0
19	71.0	41	72.6	63	77.3
20	71.1	42	72.7	64	77.7
21	71.1	43	72.8	65	78.1
22	71.2	44	72.9	66	78.4
23	71.3	45	73.0	67	78.9
24	71.3	46	73.2	68	79.3
25	71.4	47	73.3	69	79.7
26	71.5	48	73.5	70	80.2
27	71.6	49	73.6	71	80.7
28	71.6	50	73.8	72	81.2
29	71.7	51	74.0	73	81.7
30	71.8	52	74.2	74	82.2
31	71.8	53	74.4	75	82.8
32	71.9	54	74.7	76	83.3
33	72.0	55	74.9	77	83.9
34	72.0	56	75.1	78	84.5
35	72.1	57	75.4	79	85.1
36	72.2	58	75.5	80	85.7

LONGEVITY QUESTIONNAIRE TABULATION

Basic Life Expectancy (from table):——————

	YEARS SUBTRACTED	YEARS ADDED
1		
2		
3		
4		
5		
6		
7		
8		
9		
10		
11		
12		
13		
14		
15		
16		
17		
18		

TOTALS ——————————   ——————————

ACTUAL LIFE EXPECTANCY: ——————————

(Add and subtract above totals from Basic Life Expectancy)

1. Add one year for each of your grandparents who lived to be eighty or more. Add half a year for each one who topped seventy.
2. Add four years if your mother lived beyond eighty, and two if your father did so.
3. Add two years if your intelligence is above average.
4. Take off twelve years if you smoke more than forty cigarettes a day; twenty to forty, subtract seven years; less than twenty, take off two years.
5. If you enjoy sex once or twice a week, add two years.
6. If you have an annual checkup (a thorough one), add two years.
7. If you are overweight, take off two years.
8. If you sleep more than ten hours every night, or less than five, take off two years.
9. Drinking. One or two daily whiskies, half a bottle of wine, four glasses of beer—count as moderate; add three years. Light drinkers—that is, you don't drink every day—add only one and a half years. If you don't drink at all, don't add or subtract anything. Heavy drinkers and alcoholics—take off eight years.
10. Exercise. Three times a week—running, cycling, swimming, brisk walks, dancing, or skating—add three years. Don't count weekend walks, etc.
11. Do you prefer simple, plain foods, vegetables and fruit, to richer, meatier, fatty foods? If you can say yes honestly *and* stop eating before you are full, add one year.
12. If you are frequently ill, take off five years.
13. Education. If you did postgraduate work at university, add three years. For an ordinary bachelor's degree, add two. Up to grade 12, add one; grade 10 and below—none.
14. Jobs. If you are a professional person, add one and a half years; technical, managerial, administrative, and agricultural workers add one year; proprietors, clerks, and sales staff add nothing; semiskilled workers take off half a year; laborers subtract four years.

26 15. If, however, you're not a laborer but your job involves a lot
        of physical work, add two years. If it is a desk job, take
        off two.

    16. If you live in a town or have done so for most of your life,
        take off one year. Add a year if most of your time has
        been spent in the countryside.

    17. If you have one or two close friends with whom you can
        confide everything, add a year.

    18. If you are regularly able to rest, and enjoy "taking it easy,"
        add two years.

Life Expectancy Questionnaire—brief comment   27

The things you can do to change your life expectancy, should you wish to, are self-evident from the questions. We shall explore this in more detail in chapter 4 when discussing self-development.

Exercise 3. Self-analysis

This exercise, which should take you at least an hour, and may take as much as a day, involves using both the left and right side of your brain to examine *who you are now.* Using a large sheet of paper (an artist's pad is ideal), you are going to do an I-Am Mind Map of the various aspects that make up you at this moment in time. An I-Am Mind Map* uses the various elements of your left and right brain in order to give you an externalized map-picture of your thoughts on any subject; in this case your thoughts on you. The Mind Map uses images, color, visual rhythm, imagination, three dimensionality, words, numbers, logic, occasional lists, and sequencing. Before you do this exercise refer to the I-Am Mind Map on the back cover of this book.

In the center of your large blank white sheet, draw a *compact* image of either yourself or something that you feel represents yourself. Then, using as many pictures and images, and key words, as possible, develop a *complete* picture of yourself, with the key words branching off from the center, and the secondary words branching off from them and so on, much like the branches and twigs of a growing tree.

Areas that you must cover in *detail* in the self-analysis include:

1. Background
2. Strengths
3. Weaknesses
4. Hobbies
5. Accomplishments

* See the revised edition of my book *Use Both Sides of Your Brain,* 1983, for details on the Mind Map.

THE I-AM MIND MAP

(The space below has been provided for your convenience, but it would be preferable to use a larger sheet of paper, as described on page 27.)

6. Failures
7. Likes
8. Dislikes
9. Physical self-description
10. Family
11. Beliefs
12. Areas of greatest knowledge
13. Areas of greatest ignorance

Throughout this exercise, the definitions, extensions, and meanings of the words are as *you* interpret them. For example, under "Strengths" you might include your frankness, where another person might include the same quality as a weakness under "uncouth"! Be as honest and detailed as you possibly can.

Self-analysis Exercise—brief comment

If your Self-analysis Exercise has been as honest and detailed as it should be, you may have already confronted some of those "hard truths" I spoke about in chapter 1. Remember that it is in those areas that you will be able to make the greatest improvement.

Exercise 4. Your "To Do" List

Take another large sheet and note down in *detail* the things that you have to do. This should include:

· all the phone calls you have to make
· letters you have to write
· people you have to talk to
· tasks you have to accomplish
· social and business events you have to attend
· projects you have to complete, desks you have to clean

30

- files you have to update
- things you have to review
- books you have to read
- subscriptions you have to make or cancel
- financial affairs you have to straighten out
- people you have to apologize to
- anniversaries and birthdays you have to remember
- etc.

In addition to these detailed areas, include more general areas, such as habits you want to change, long-term goals, etc.

Make sure that this list is exhaustive. The first burst of ideas may take between half an hour and an hour, but other items may pop up from time to time before you move on to the final exercise, "Your Ideal Future." Give yourself a maximum of two days for this exercise.

And don't forget that one of the "to dos" is occasionally to "not do"—to allow right-brain breaks and serendipity! Don't ignore your right-brain agenda!

My "To-Do" List

My "To-Do" List

My "To-Do" List

My "To-Do" List

Your "To-Do" List may look daunting. But even if the four pages included were not quite enough for you, you will find it all manageable once you learn about chunking in chapter 4.

Exercise 5. Your Ideal Future

Let your right brain go! Imagine that you have limitless time, resources, and energy, and that you can do *anything* that you wish for all eternity. Again, using a large sheet of blank paper, and having a compact image in the center that pictures for you the essence of your Ideal Future, develop a Mind Map (or ten!) on all those things you would like to accomplish if there were no bounds placed upon your imagination and capacity. In this Mind Map should be included all those ghost hobbies that have been waiting for expression, as well as any other dream you may have had for yourself.

Spend at least an hour on this exercise and use as much of your right-brain color and imagination as possible. This section should include all your secret "if only . . ." desires. It should also include those things you *really* would like to do; a number of people jot down "seducing the entire population of the opposite sex," but when examining whether they would really want to do so, find, often to their surprise, that they would not.

MY IDEAL FUTURE

Your Ideal Future—brief comment

After making your Mind Map, edit it down to what can be real-
istically accomplished in the time left to you (see Life Expectancy Questionnaire).

4

Divide
and Conquer

Now that you have gathered information on your past, your present, and your future, you are going to do a new, in-depth analysis of yourself using the power of your mind to "chunk," to integrate and organize.

To demonstrate the natural tendency of your brain to chunk, and also to find the natural limits and boundaries for this capacity, do the following two exercises, reading the instructions carefully, and analyzing your own mental processes as you progress step-by-step through the exercise.

Exercise 1. List memory

Following these instructions is a long list of words. The list is too long for you to remember all of it, so the task is simply to read the words one by one, at your normal reading pace, *without looking back*, memorizing as many of the words as you can, in order,

38 carefully examining the process of your mind as you go through the exercise. This means you should be aware of any difficulties you experience, of your successes, of any techniques you naturally use, and any other observations you have about how *your* brain tackles such a task. When you have finished reading the list, *immediately* turn to page 40 and write down as many of the words as you can, as well as your own observations on your mental and emotional processes throughout the test.

Cat

Leaf

Sun

House

Sky

Shoe

Student

Orange

Watch

Color

Glass

Road

Tree

Pencil

Flower

Table

Tooth

Water

Paper

Rock

Plastic

Present

Carpet

Garden

Book

LIST MEMORY EXERCISE RESULTS

1. Words in order that you were able to remember.

_____

_____

_____

_____

_____

_____

_____

_____

2. Your mental and emotional processes during the exercise.

_____

_____

_____

_____

_____

_____

_____

_____

Exercise 2. Number/calculation/memory exercise

This exercise involves *mental* arithmetic, and it is important that you *do not* write down any of your calculations. Following is a list of mental additions. In each case read the question once; then, *without looking back*, do the calculation in your head. When you have completed one calculation, move on to the next. Again, as in the previous exercise, examine in detail the processes of your brain as you perform the calculations, including any emotional reactions, mental blocking, etc. When you reach a question that you find too difficult to handle, consider the exercise finished, and turn back to page 40, where you should note down your mental processes during this mathematics exercise as well as any emotional reactions you experienced. Remember, *don't* write down your calculations; this must be an entirely mental exercise.

1. One plus three = _____
2. Nine plus twelve = _____
3. Thirty-one plus forty-seven = _____
4. Eighty-five plus fifty-six = _____
5. One hundred & thirteen plus forty-nine = _____
6. One hundred & sixty-seven plus one hundred & thirty-eight = _____
7. Nine hundred & thirty-three plus seven hundred & eighty-nine = _____
8. One thousand two hundred & forty-two plus three thousand seven hundred and fifty-seven = _____
9. Four thousand nine hundred & eighty-seven plus nine thousand eight hundred & seventy-four = _____
10. Thirteen thousand seven hundred & sixty-three plus fifteen thousand seven hundred & eighty-seven = _____
11. Eighty-seven thousand five hundred & ninety-six point three nine plus seventy-four thousand three hundred & eighty-nine point eight nine = _____

Chunking exercise analysis

In the first exercise most people find themselves remembering the first few words, perhaps a couple of the last words, plus any other words that were particularly significant to them, or that in some way could be linked to a meaningful association or story. Of the first words remembered, very few people get more than seven in a row correct. Similarly, other linkage-associations tend very seldom to number more than seven.

What this demonstrates is that there seems to be a natural barrier at around the number seven for the number of things that our brains can "hold in suspension." Past this point, the only way we can avoid losing control of things is by "fixing them" externally.

Similarly, in the addition test, although all the sums would have been easy had they been written down, most people come unstuck before the last one. As they become progressively more difficult, there is just too much individual data to juggle without the structure falling apart.

Throughout both exercises you may have felt apprehensive, increasingly frustrated as the difficulty increased, and generally out of control because in some way you failed.

Everybody does fail.

And it is the same in life. We fail not because we lack the basic ability to succeed, but because we do not take into account the brain's natural organizing and chunking processes. As a consequence we usually tend to juggle too many different "sections of ourselves" at the same time, until we eventually lose control either by having some form of breakdown, by giving up, or by mistakingly feeling that we are inadequate.

Common sense dictates that, in the limited time available to us, we need to restrict those "sections of ourselves" to a reasonable number. Identifying these sections *and* writing them down makes it easier for you to juggle them mentally than in the unaided exercises 1 and 2. If you have reasonably restricted the number of sections, they will be more easily remembered, cate-

gorized, and handled when you are away from the notes in your 43
self-management system.

Gaining control of yourself

In order to gain more control of your own life, you are next going to divide yourself into seven or fewer Major Divisions, thus allowing you to utilize the natural tendencies and capacities of your brain. This will further enable you to get a clear perspective of who you actually are and of who you wish to become.

While you are establishing your Major Divisions, bear constantly in mind that the left and right sides of your brain should be balanced, that your brain needs activity *and* rest, that your recall and understanding are different and therefore need careful time management, and that you need provision for pace change and serendipity. Remember also that organization allows you a real freedom, and that disorganized chaos is in fact one of the worst and most subtle forms of prison.

Exercise 3. Self-chunking

The I-Am Mind Map

Carefully analyze your I-Am Mind Map, noting the Major Divisions of your life. If there are more than seven, blend some of them into single categories (for example, "running" and "diet" could be combined under the heading "health"). At the end of this exercise you should have divided your present self into seven or fewer categories. Start now:

1. _____

2. _____

44 3. _____

4. _____

5. _____

6. _____

7. _____

"To Do" List

As with your I-Am Mind Map, divide your "To Do" List into seven or fewer Major Divisions.

Start now:

1. _____

2. _____

3. _____

4. _____

5. _____

6. _____

7. _____

The Ideal-Future Mind Map

As with the previous two exercises, divide your Ideal Future into seven or fewer Major Divisions:

1. _____

2. _____

3. _____

4. _____

5. _____

6. _____

7. _____

Integration

On the next page note the seven Major Divisions from your I-Am Mind Map, your "To Do" List, and your Ideal-Future Mind Map. Finally, blend them into the seven or fewer Major Divisions that make up your life as you are at the moment, including what you have to do and what you wish to be.

Don't worry about a "perfect list," as the seven or fewer categories that you choose at this stage may well be adjusted even before you have finished the book. To help you select, samples of Major Divisions chosen by people in my seminars are outlined on the following page.

In addition, the following sections on the need for love and friendship, self-development, and financial self-management are also included to give you guidelines and suggestions for selecting your Major Divisions. If you wish to complete this exercise after having read these sections, by all means do so. On the other hand you may wish to complete the exercise first, then read the sections, and subsequently make adjustments.

SELF-CHUNKING: SEVEN MAJOR DIVISIONS

Home	Study	Community
Family	Culture	Reading
Work	Learning	Emotional Stabilizing
Quality of life	Travel	Sensuality
Children	Play	Sexuality
Running	Creativity	Writing
Business	Money	Loving
Religion	Law	Games
Friends	House	Pets
Leisure	Finance	Food
Hobbies	Accounts	Nutrition
Relaxation	Entertainment	Environment
Holidays	Self-improvement	
Sports	Self-development	
Social	Spiritual	

The need for love and friendship

Recent studies of the brain have shown that it requires four basic foods:

1. Nutrition
2. Oxygen
3. Information
4. Love and affection

Without this last "food" many laboratory animals were found to die within a very short period of time, even though they were well fed and exercised. With human beings it is even more complex and serious, since for us love takes many forms, including brotherly, sexual, and spiritual.

To help you realize how important it is for you, examine your own reactions when love has been taken away from you, and you will probably find either a tendency toward tremendous

48   and immediate hurt, pain, and despair, or an opposite tendency toward a steel-hard reaction of defense/aggression. Both reactions indicate the importance of this basic human need, and it is vital that in your seven divisions you have one area devoted to this or to something similar. It might be headed "Family," "Friends," "Family and Friends," or "Loving Relationships," etc., but whatever it is, you (and your loved ones) need it.

You might be wondering why love should be included in a book on self-management based on the brain. Love is included because your brain, not your heart, is the center of your emotions, and if it is satisfied in the area of love, most other aspects of your self-management will automatically slot neatly into place.

An example of where knowledge of your brain, time management, and personal planning weave nicely together can be found on many people's doorsteps!

In the stereotypical situation, the husband, who has been working all day (the predominantly left-brain activities of reading, writing, analyzing, thinking, and talking), arrives exhausted on the doorstep, to be greeted by his wife who has also been working (but in a more right-brain mode: cooking, ironing, listening to the radio while she cleans the house, and shopping). All he wants to do is collapse into a chair with a drink and to give his left brain a good rest. Since her left brain has been starved for much of the day, all she wants to do is talk, exchange ideas, and give her right brain a rest. The result is often an explosion, in which he accuses her of nagging, pestering, and constantly talking, while she accuses him of inconsideration, lack of appreciation for all she does for him, and being an uncommunicative slob!

Such situations can often lead to the complete breakdown of a relationship, whereas a simple understanding of the way in which the two persons' brains are operating would help diminish the danger.

The Buffer Zone

In situations like the one described above, the "Buffer Zone" is the ideal solution. The Buffer Zone is a time between your actual physical meeting and your real mental getting-together, where each of you allows the other a time-space in order for your brains to settle down and become more balanced. It is much like the diving or space decompression chamber, where the body becomes adjusted to different pressures of air and water. This Buffer Zone also provides the opportunity for both people to get out of themselves. Allowing this freedom is a large part of what love is all about.

The Buffer Zone can also be applied at work. In one study completed in my own organization, it was found that the secretaries found themselves constantly unable to complete their day's work satisfactorily because of constant interruptions from the phone and from people asking them to do unexpected tasks. This led to a feeling of dissatisfaction and general frustration. As a joint project, we broke down and analyzed the hours they actually spent on various tasks during their day and found that on average two hours were spent on the interruptions they had correctly identified.

From that time on we planned the secretaries' day to include a two-hour Buffer Zone for the necessary and inevitable interruptions. With this new method of planning, any phone call or unexpected task became expected, and therefore acceptable, rather than resented as an unnecessary and annoying interruption. The result of this change was an enormous improvement in personal relationships.

Self-development

Another highly recommended area for one of your seven or fewer Major Divisions is that of self-development. In consid-

50 ering this area it is important that you bear in mind two of the other main "brain foods": oxygen and information.

Your brain and physical health (heart-training exercises)

Although your brain weighs only three and a half pounds, which is usually somewhere between one and three percent of your entire body weight, it *consumes* twenty percent of the oxygen intake (this oxygen reacts with other chemicals to provide your energy). This is because your *billions* of brain cells are constantly undergoing fantastically complex electrochemical changes as they process the enormous amount of information that constantly pours through you.

If you wish to maintain the efficient operation of this entire system, it is important to make sure that a regular supply of fresh oxygen is provided, and one of the best ways of accomplishing this is to embark on a basic program of aerobic (oxygen supply) fitness. This can take many forms, and should be an activity that is both interesting and personally stimulating to you. The most effective aerobic activities include the following:

Running and jogging
Swimming
Bicycling
Cross-country skiing
Aerobic, athletic, and discotheque dancing
Strenuous hiking or climbing
Active and prolonged lovemaking
Squash
Skipping rope

These are not the only effective aerobic exercises, and any that you are familiar with or have devised yourself that can keep your heart pumping at approximately 120+ beats a minute for twenty minutes at least three times a week will provide you with the "oxygen food" that you need. In addition to supplying your brain with this extra energy, you will notice that such an inclusion in your self-development program increases overall intelligence and creativity, reduces stress, increases stamina, and leads to general well-being.

The physical maintenance and development program is essential to your well-being. You should embark upon it immediately.

Considering your Life Expectancy Questionnaire

If part of your goal is to live a happy, healthy, and long life, then checking the Life Expectancy Questionnaire can provide useful information to guide your future activity.

To run through them quickly, the following are brief ideas on improving life expectancy by improving your mental and physical activity:

* Your intelligence can be improved by using your left and right brains together, and by increasing your vocabulary.
* If you smoke, both physical and mental health can be improved by either cutting down or stopping the habit.
* Yes, make sure that you include time for lovemaking. Because this seems so obvious, many people both in their planning and in their day-to-day, nonplanned lives tend to assume it, and in assuming, neglect it.
* Plan for a regular medical checkup, try to maintain a reasonable weight, and make sure you get a reasonable amount of sleep.
* Drinking seems to be OK, as long as it's in moderation (and you don't experiment too frequently with right-brain imagination/alcohol exercises!).
* Exercise, as I have previously indicated, is exceptionally important and should be a major part of your self-development program.
* A simple, relatively plain, vegetable- and fruit-dominated diet will keep you both mentally and physically alert.

52

* If your education is not as complete as you would like, plan, in a balanced-brain way, to expand it, for it will lengthen your life.
* Make sure that your job includes a reasonable balance of mental and physical activity; make sure you spend time in the country (it's good for the right brain as well as the lungs!).
* If you do not have a close friend, a program of balancing your personality as we've outlined will improve your chances of forming those special and important bonds with others.
* Once again, make sure you get regular rests and are able to enjoy yourself when you take it easy.

The Life Expectancy Questionnaire, devised by actuaries, leads to conclusions that are identical with those of brain and body research.

Vocabulary improvement

Another subdivision in your self-development section should be regular vocabulary improvement. This mental area has been found to have one of the highest correlations with business, economic, and intellectual success, and is easily accomplished. The reason for this high correlation lies in the fact that a developed vocabulary allows you to expand automatically your abilities in conceptualization, analysis, logic, and sequencing—all left-brain attributes that are highly prized in society.

As this skill continues to develop, it can connect to right-hemisphere activities. In addition to increasing your logical capabilities, the words will begin to link more readily into images and the realm of creative imagination. Vocabulary skill is easily acquired, and, as mentioned before, raises your intelligence quotient.

There are many excellent vocabulary improvement books on the market today and you can supplement these by developing an interest in all those words you encounter whose definitions you do not *fully* know. Make a commitment to jot these down whenever you come across them. Look them up in a dictionary as soon as possible, and then use them three or four times the following day. In this manner your vocabulary will increase significantly week by week. As it does, so will your ability to communicate, to express yourself, and to clearly define your thoughts, emotions, and goals.

Other subdivisions in the self-development section which have proved popular, and from which you might select another two or three, include the following:

> Musical instruments to play
> Board game skills to acquire
> Riding or driving skills to acquire
> Books to read
> Questions to explore
> Knowledge to acquire
> Facts and data to record and remember
> Films and theater to see
> Ideas to develop
> Jokes to remember and develop the skill for telling
> Languages to learn
> Music to listen to, learn about, and become expert in
> Quotes to record and remember
> Logical debating and arguing skills to acquire
> Mechanical and physical skills to develop
> Emotional and interpersonal areas to enhance

In dividing your self-development section into its subdivisions, remember the rule of seven. Avoid the tendency to become overenthusiastic. Don't try to become Leonardo da Vinci in a day! Give yourself a reasonable number of self-development goals to begin with, and build on them only when your initial skills are acquired and your initial goals in this area accomplished.

54   If you wish to specifically develop vocabulary skills, there are four optional vocabulary building pages at the back of the Major Division section in this book (pp. 119–122).

Financial self-management

The third necessary area in your seven or fewer Major Divisions is that of financial self-management. It is the area where the most fear is generally experienced. Many people get into trouble because they are reluctant to look at their financial facts. They assume that things will generally sort themselves out but live in constant fear of bills, credit card accumulations, and those unforeseen debts that can strike out of the blue. Even people in the highest positions, earning large salaries, can invite disaster through inadequate financial planning.

One friend of mine, the managing director of a major United States organization, received a phone call one morning from his son at college informing him that the university registrar had said that he was not allowed to attend classes because his father had neglected to pay that year's tuition! The fee in this case was $9,000. As it turned out, the father was able to pay the amount. Nevertheless, it came as a considerable blow to him, as he had not given enough consideration to detailed budget planning. The shock of the event left him in constant apprehension that something similar would happen in the future.

It is essential that you incorporate into your self-management system a carefully considered budget that includes Cash Flow—the consideration not only of how much you have earned, but also of when you are going to receive those monies that you have earned. Your Cash Flow also considers when you are going to have to pay those monies that you owe. This will give you a clear picture of the energy flow of your resources and will enable you to decide more consciously just where you wish to spend the money you have earned.

It is important at this stage of your planning to realize that money is not a threat or some mysterious mathematical monster that occasionally comes to harass you. It is *energy* that you work to acquire, and which, if you manage it well, can provide you with even *more* energy. In one recent survey it was found that approximately ninety-five percent of people tend to shy away from any *real* looking at their financial resources. But when they did begin to look, enormous amounts of stress were eliminated, and a more appropriate and beneficial use of money-energy often resulted.

If you have not already done any basic financial analysis of your situation, complete the exercises on the following pages.

Financial analysis

WHAT I POSSESS

On this page list everything that you own that is worth money, with its estimated cash value, as well as any cash or positive bank balances you have.

POSSESSION	VALUE

TOTAL _____

WHAT I OWE

On this page itemize all your outstanding debts.

DEBTS	AMOUNT

TOTAL _____

Cash Flow Forecast

On the following page is a Cash Flow Forecast sheet which will allow you to work out your first rough Cash Flow Forecast. Cash Flow is usually worked out over a period of twelve months and is divided into two major areas: your income and your expenses. In the upper section, make a note of the various sources of your income and when you *expect to receive* the monies owed to you. Sources of income might include salaries, odd jobs, commissions, gifts, royalties, and so on. When you have entered these for each of the twelve months, add up your total income for the period, then add that to your expected bank balance for that month (assuming your balance is positive), and calculate the total.

Next, consider your expenditures for each month. Expenditures should include such items as rent and rates, heating and power, tax, entertainment, car, travel and holidays, and self-development, etc. When you have completed all your entries, total your expenses for each month, adjust that to your opening bank balance (if it's in debit), and again calculate the total. Then for each month calculate the difference between B and D, which will show you how much money you actually have at the end of that month, regardless of what you still owe or are still owed.

Once you begin to see this financial flow chart more clearly, you will be able to make a number of important decisions about how and where you earn your money; how you actually spend what you earn; where you need to strengthen or pare down; and where and how you can adjust your income and expenses to attain the goals you have set yourself in life.

Managing your Cash Flow can actually change and improve your life. Consider a friend of mine in New York who lived on a regular monthly income of $3,000, which he considered a *minimal* requirement for his existence. Recently he took the opportunity of traveling around Europe with a companion for one year, on a budget of $11,000!

My friend had always been reluctant to get involved with financial planning, but the circumstances forced him to, and of the two he became the group accountant. He broke the money down into monthly and weekly amounts, calculated essential expenses, and kept himself and his friend on an almost military financial regimen. To his amazement the living was actually easy, and on certain weeks he managed to keep below budget. On such weeks the "reward" was a special meal in a restaurant. The two also found that at certain times the budget would not allow them to take long motor trips that they had wished to take, because the gasoline was too expensive. As a result, they were occasionally obliged to stay put in certain areas of Europe and regularly found that these "serendipitous" experiences were among the highlights of the tour!

Once you have your basic finances under control you may find that you have, or are going to have, certain resources left over. Such a surplus would enable you to decide the right buying times for things (for example, sales, seasonal fluctuations, etc.). It would also enable you to invest. Such investment is a major area of study in itself, but on a simple basis it can be normally divided into three parts:

1. Essential savings, which you are building up for some long-term purpose and which you refuse to risk
2. Basic reserves, which are those resources you wish to have available for any emergencies but which you are willing to let grow, with perhaps some slight risk
3. Venture capital, which, depending upon how much of a gambler you are, you are willing to invest at a higher risk, in the hope of a substantial return

Your Cash Flow Forecast will be the basis on which you explore these possibilities.

CASH FLOW FORECAST

Month				
Income sources				
Total income for period				
Opening bank balance (if in credit)　A				
TOTAL　B				
Expenditure				
Total expenditure for period				
Opening bank balance (if in debt)　C				
TOTAL　D				
Difference between B and D*				

* Show as Credit or Debit and carry forward to next column against A or C as appropriate.

								TOTAL FOR WHOLE PERIOD

Selecting your remaining divisions

I have recommended that in your Life Management Program you have at least one division for love, one for self-development (and its various important subdivisions), and one for financial self-management. These three divisions may cover the entire spectrum of your life. If, however, after considering who you are, what you can do, and what you wish to become, there are still things which these three areas do not cover, then you need to select other areas to complete the whole picture of yourself.

When you have completed the selection of these areas, it is important that together they represent the *complete* picture of who you are, without any omissions. It is also important to make sure that each area is clearly defined and that you do not reserve the seventh division for "odds and ends." Such a division, due to time pressure, procrastination, occasional tendencies toward laziness, etc., tends to be the barrel into which every item which would require a moment of thought for classification gets thrown. It gradually becomes the bulk of your system and forces you back into your earlier disorganized state. It may be useful now to refer once again to the division headings that people from my seminars have chosen. Many of the headings appear to be quite similar, but the shades of difference in their meaning are important.

When completing the selection of your Major Divisions, "listen" to *all* the various tunes that go to make up the symphony of yourself. And don't worry about picking the "wrong" titles. The divisions you choose may (and in most cases do) change as your life progresses. In my own case, for instance, I have modified my Major Divisions five times in the last three years.

For example, I changed the ranking of my legal and finance section from seventh to fifth when I realized I was not paying enough attention to it. I blended my two separate divisions of "Family" and "Friends" into one division when I realized that to -me they were all "Family." And I eliminated a section entitled

"Projects" when it became obvious to me that each one of the   63
projects comfortably slotted into my other Major Divisions.

Exercise 4. Ranking reality; ranking ideal

Now that you have chosen your seven or fewer Major Divisions,
rank them in order of importance in the space provided below:

1. _____

2. _____

3. _____

4. _____

5. _____

6. _____

7. _____

Now, assuming that you have one hundred percent of your time
to devote to them, give each area its *ideal* percentage—in other
words, the percentage of your time you would ideally like to
devote to each of these areas:

	DIVISION	% RANK (IDEAL)
1.		
2.		
3.		
4.		
5.		
6.		
7.		

64   Now assign a percentage for the amount of time you *actually*
spend on average in each division:

DIVISION	% RANK (REAL)
1.	
2.	
3.	
4.	
5.	
6.	
7.	

Finally, compare your ideal with your real life, noting in the column provided the percentage difference—for example, if for
family and friends your ideal percentage was forty and your actual percentage ten, then the difference is thirty.

DIVISION	IDEAL	REAL	DIFFERENCE
1.			
2.			
3.			
4.			
5.			
6.			
7.			

The purpose of this exercise is to examine the difference between your real and your ideal life, and to allow you to change
the pattern so that the real more closely approximates (although

it may never actually reach) the ideal. Those who have done this exercise find that the areas in their life where they are currently experiencing the most difficulties usually include:

1. The area they have ranked lowest
2. The areas where there are greatest discrepancies between the ideal and the real
3. The areas where they had confusion sorting out percentage estimations

The reason why it is useful for you to have this information is that your brain is a self-correcting organ and works much like a guided spaceship: as long as it has its planetary target, and as long as it "knows" when it is going off target, it will automatically realign its path, constantly zeroing in more accurately on the desired target. If you therefore find yourself with major discrepancies, don't be discouraged. Your brain will automatically register these on the conscious and subconscious level, and will start its own self-correcting program, aided by your conscious self-management.

Organizing your seven or fewer Major Divisions

The next part of *The Brain User's Guide* consists of seven sections to help you with the detailed organization of your Major Divisions. Each of these seven sections is divided as follows:

1. *Image page.* For each of your Major Divisions it is important to have an image that you have either drawn or selected from your own photography collection or from a book or magazine—an illustration that epitomizes for you the subject matter of that particular area. For example, for the self-development section you might have an image similar to the one illustrated in figures 3 or 4.

   The function of this image is to trigger the imaginative right side of your brain and to give you a mental set

66

that allows your self-correcting brain to aim constantly at an ideal. This is a technique used by many of the great and successful people of past and current generations, including Albert Einstein, John D. Rockefeller, Henry Ford, Mohammed Ali, Bjorn Borg, Theodore Roosevelt, Wilbur Wright, Woodrow Wilson, Alexander Graham Bell, and Gary Player. The image gives you pleasure whenever you see it, which draws your mind's associations more positively toward that which you wish to accomplish.

If you have the skill and/or the courage, it is advisable to draw your own image, for this gets the networks of your mind more "involved." As time progresses it will encourage you to improve the image, at the same time improving your skill in art, a skill which itself feeds back to the right side of the brain, producing an overall development.

FIG. 3. SELF-IMAGE

FIG. 4. SELF-IMAGE

At your leisure, turn to the image page of each of the Major Divisions, completing your ideal image for each one.

2. *Major subdivisions.* When you have completed your image for each Major Division, you will be ready to divide each division into seven or fewer subdivisions. You have already started to do this with your self-development division and can now continue in each of the other Major Divisions (pages 70–118). At this stage some people protest that there is no way in which they can do this, because they have far too much to accomplish in each division. If this is the case, it may well mean your life is running away from you. The fact is that there simply isn't the time in the average life to cope with more than seven subdivisions of seven Major Divisions.

3. *Major goals.* Next, on page 3 of each section, complete, either in image form, in Mind Map form, or in list-of-

68   priority order form, the major goals you wish to accomplish in each of your Major Divisions. Beside each major goal put a rough estimate of the date on which you would like to have accomplished that goal. (I have yet to meet anyone who has been one hundred percent successful in this estimation; as with the percentage rankings, it is a question of starting off on the path toward the ideal and allowing your brain to direct you, with its trial-and-error mechanism, toward the goal.)

4, 5, 6, 7. *Particular goals and dates.* In each Major Division, the fourth through seventh pages are for listing in chronological order the *particular* goals you wish to accomplish. This will enable you to keep a year-long check on your progress.

    Failure to meet all of these immediate goals is in no way a disaster; it is, in fact, common. When goals are not met, reassessment and reevaluation are required, and a more realistic date and/or more realistic goal can be set. In some instances, time pressure and changes in your life may actually mean the useful discarding of certain goals.

    While you complete each of these goal pages, bear in mind the fact that this is *your* life and that you arrange it as *you* wish. Your picture of your ideal life will be different from everyone else's. If, for example, certain aspects of your behavior reduce your life expectancy and you accept that knowingly, then that is your own personal choice and not something you "must" or "must not" do.

    Similarly, be aware of the fact that your first subdividing, first ranking, and first goal setting will be just that—your first. As time progresses and the nature and tenor of your life changes and develops, so will the importance you place on individual divisions. Certain divisions will become less significant or perhaps even disappear; other divisions which do not exist at the moment

may suddenly enter and even come to dominate your
life.

When you have completed this exercise (pages 70–118), your Life Management Program will be complete. It will then be up to you to use it to the best of your advantage. The final chapter includes recommendations for blending the program with your day-to-day life.

IMAGE PAGE

MAJOR SUBDIVISIONS

MAJOR GOALS

Particular Goals and Dates

GOAL	DATE TO BE ACCOMPLISHED

PARTICULAR GOALS AND DATES

GOAL   DATE

PARTICULAR GOALS AND DATES

GOAL	DATE

Particular Goals and Dates

GOAL	DATE

MAJOR DIVISION TWO

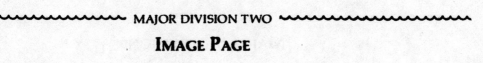

IMAGE PAGE

MAJOR SUBDIVISIONS

MAJOR GOALS

Particular Goals and Dates

GOAL	DATE

Particular Goals and Dates

GOAL	DATE

Particular Goals and Dates

GOAL	DATE

PARTICULAR GOALS AND DATES

GOAL	DATE

IMAGE PAGE

MAJOR SUBDIVISIONS

MAJOR GOALS

Particular Goals and Dates

GOAL	DATE

PARTICULAR GOALS AND DATES

GOAL	DATE

PARTICULAR GOALS AND DATES

GOAL	DATE

PARTICULAR GOALS AND DATES

GOAL	DATE

GOAL	DATE

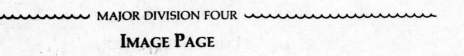

IMAGE PAGE

MAJOR SUBDIVISIONS

Major Goals

Particular Goals and Dates

GOAL	DATE

Particular Goals and Dates

GOAL	DATE

PARTICULAR GOALS AND DATES

GOAL	DATE

PARTICULAR GOALS AND DATES

GOAL	DATE

IMAGE PAGE

MAJOR SUBDIVISIONS

MAJOR GOALS

Particular Goals and Dates

GOAL	DATE

PARTICULAR GOALS AND DATES

GOAL	DATE

PARTICULAR GOALS AND DATES

GOAL	DATE

PARTICULAR GOALS AND DATES

GOAL	DATE

IMAGE PAGE

MAJOR SUBDIVISIONS

MAJOR GOALS

PARTICULAR GOALS AND DATES

GOAL	DATE

PARTICULAR GOALS AND DATES

GOAL	DATE

Particular Goals and Dates

GOAL	DATE

Particular Goals and Dates

GOAL	DATE

IMAGE PAGE

MAJOR SUBDIVISIONS

MAJOR GOALS

Particular Goals and Dates

GOAL	DATE

PARTICULAR GOALS AND DATES

GOAL	DATE

PARTICULAR GOALS AND DATES

GOAL	DATE

PARTICULAR GOALS AND DATES

GOAL	DATE

Vocabulary Improvement

WORD	DEFINITION

Vocabulary Improvement

WORD	DEFINITION

Vocabulary Improvement

WORD	DEFINITION

Vocabulary Improvement

WORD | DEFINITION

5

Advice for
the Future

Now that you have completed your self-examination, a more positive and more manageable future lies ahead of you. Your newly defined goals and aspirations can be woven into the fabric of your daily life, nurturing and improving your existence. In order to assist yourself in this, it is advisable to monitor your goals, which are like New Year's resolutions, which in this case you must make four times a year.

Next, go to your current diary and make dates with yourself approximately three months from today, six months from today, nine months from today, and twelve months from today. On these dates you will spend *at least* half a day monitoring and checking all the pages in your self-management system. Remember as you do so that the existence of unachieved goals is not a failure but simply another signpost on the pathway toward the eventual realization of your goals. The four sheets following this page are your quarterly review sheets, where you can easily record your accomplishments.

124   After you have made these dates with yourself, spend *at least* three hours with your *Brain User's Guide* and all your diary and calendar systems, reviewing your Major Division images, your Major Subdivisions, your Major Goals, and your Particular Goals and Dates. Transfer the most important Particular Goals into the appropriate date sections of your diary systems, thus giving you, as you end your first reading of this book, a *definite plan* of action for the future. The commitments you have made three months, six months, nine months, and twelve months from today will guarantee that this plan and your goals will be realized.

On those days when you are monitoring and checking the pages in your self-management system, also quickly review your *Brain User's Guide* in order to reinforce the information so essential for the better functioning of your brain.

REVIEW AND SELF-MONITORING PAGE

GOALS ACCOMPLISHED	ORIGINAL DATE SET	ACTUAL DATE ACCOMPLISHED

GOALS NOT ACCOMPLISHED	ORIGINAL DATE	NEW DATE

Review and Self-Monitoring Page

GOALS ACCOMPLISHED	ORIGINAL DATE SET	ACTUAL DATE ACCOMPLISHED

GOALS NOT ACCOMPLISHED	ORIGINAL DATE	NEW DATE

Review and Self-Monitoring Page

GOALS ACCOMPLISHED	ORIGINAL DATE SET	ACTUAL DATE ACCOMPLISHED

GOALS NOT ACCOMPLISHED	ORIGINAL DATE	NEW DATE

Review and Self-Monitoring Page

GOALS ACCOMPLISHED	ORIGINAL DATE SET	ACTUAL DATE ACCOMPLISHED

GOALS NOT ACCOMPLISHED	ORIGINAL DATE	NEW DATE

IN CONCLUSION

From this day on *The Brain User's Guide* can be the basis for your continuing self-monitoring and establishment of goals; it will be a constant reminder of the vast range of skills that your brain actually possesses.

The information on the brain will have helped you realize that there are certain things about yourself it is both essential and encouraging for you to understand. You will have learned that life is best lived with *both* natural discipline *and* freedom, and that these two concepts are complementary and mutually supporting.

Now that you are more aware of who you were, who you are, and what you have to do, the future will allow you to become that person you wish to be.

My best wishes for your success.